THE CRAZY WORLD OF CATS

CARTOONS BY

Buisott

▤ EXLEY

Other cartoon giftbooks in this series:
The Crazy World of Football (Bill Stott)
The Crazy World of Gardening (Bill Stott)
The Crazy World of Golf (Mike Scott)
The Crazy World of Housework (Bill Stott)
The Crazy World of Marriage (Bill Stott)
The Crazy World of Rugby (Bill Stott)
The Crazy World of Sex (Bill Stott)

First published in hardback in the USA in 1996 by Exley Giftbooks.
Published in Great Britain in 1996 by Exley Publications Ltd.

12 11 10 9 8 7 6

Printed in China.

Exley Publications Ltd, 16 Chalk Hill, Watford, Herts WD19 4BG, UK.
Exley Publications LLC, 185 Main Street, Spencer, MA 01562, USA.
www.helenexleygiftbooks.com

"I think that hairdryer is too powerful for him..."

"All that stuff about bringing them gifts – it's rubbish.
We do it just to scare them!"

"Oh, come, come – does she look like a cat who'd make a smell?"

"O.K. a brief explanation will do.
Why is my chicken leg in <u>your</u> mouth?"

"An ultimate deterrent eh? Don't make me laugh fellas."

"You must tell me if he's being a nuisance..."

"How come <u>I</u> get thrown out when the flea was found on the <u>carpet</u>?"

"You're sitting in his chair..."

"Hey! There's wild life on this set!"

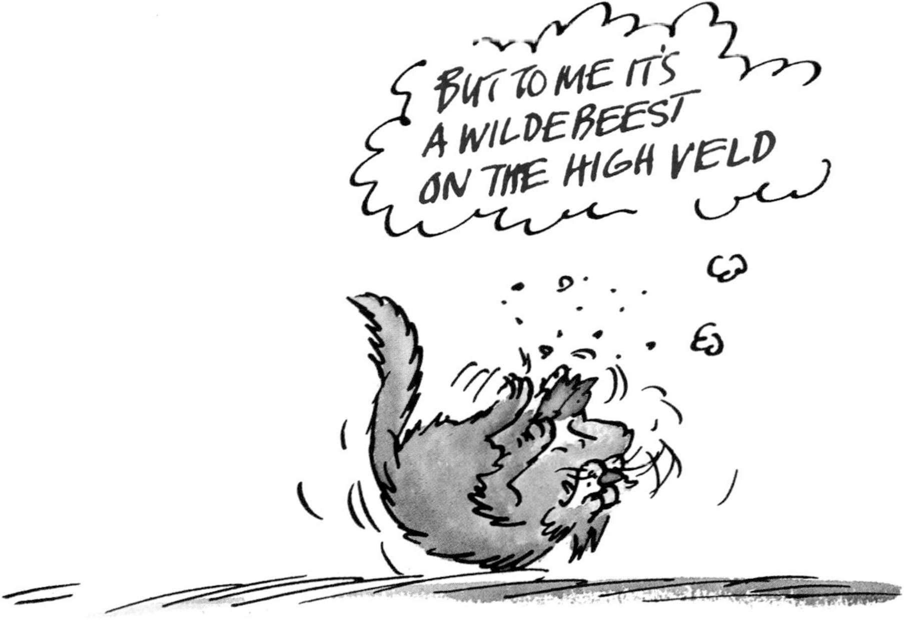
BUT TO ME IT'S A WILDEBEEST ON THE HIGH VELD

"Gran! Oscar doesn't seem too keen on 'Kittichews'."

"Don't be alarmed. It's just his way of saying
'please don't hurt me.'"

"Play with the yarn. Don't kill it!"

"What a coward! He's telling me the canary
clawed the couch."

"This way I get all the excitement of the flying boot with
none of the effort..."

"That's what I call a cat flap!"

"Normally I'd have to admit you're a pretty hum-drum
kind of guy. But with that can-opener in your hand,
you're a giant."

"Well, of course she's growling. You put ketchup on your
steak and she hates ketchup."

"The twins tried out your home perm kit on Chester."

URRRRR···

POUNCE!

"And when she actually deigns to come home, we'll do our tiger ambush!"

2 "It's as I suspected – the oaf doesn't speak Felinese!"

"So much for your independence act!"

"What did the nasty man do to mama's little soldier?"

"You can tell he's a pedigree. He's the only member of the family who likes politics."

"I can't teach her that she's not meant to bath in it!"

"Remember the bird we nearly caught this morning?
He's back – with his big brother..."

"Here Smelly, Smelly. Here Smelly..."

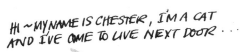

2

"Harold! Quick! The screens!"

I KNOW, I KNOW — IT'S A SCRATCH POST. I STILL PREFER THE WALLPAPER · · · ·

"Don't worry about a thing – I had the operation..."

"Learning to climb trees is cheating!"

"What's wrong? He always washes that way – don't they all?"

"Satisfy my curiosity – if you could get at me, would you actually eat me?"

"A simple 'yes' or 'no' will do."

"How many times do I have to tell you? Never change
channels without asking – it's very rude..."

"Louie, I'd better hang up. They're staring at me the way
they always do when I use the 'phone."

"How'd you like it if I came and lay on <u>your</u> chest
first thing in the morning?"

"I'll wait until someone comes by before I go and have a drink.
I just love those cries of middle class outrage."

"Either you come in right now or you're out all night!"

Books in the "Crazy World" series

The Crazy World of Cats (Bill Stott)
The Crazy World of Football (Bill Stott)
The Crazy World of Gardening (Bill Stott)
The Crazy World of Golf (Mike Scott)
The Crazy World of Housework (Bill Stott)
The Crazy World of Marriage (Bill Stott)
The Crazy World of Rugby (Bill Stott)
The Crazy World of Sex (Bill Stott)

Books in the "Fanatic's" series

The Fanatic's Guides are perfect presents for
everyone with a hobby that has got out of hand.
Over fifty hilarious colour cartoons by Roland Fiddy.

The Fanatic's Guide to Cats
The Fanatic's Guide to Computers
The Fanatic's Guide to Dads
The Fanatic's Guide to D.I.Y.
The Fanatic's Guide to Golf
The Fanatic's Guide to Husbands
The Fanatic's Guide to Love
The Fanatic's Guide to Sex

Great Britain: Order these super books from
your local bookseller or from Exley Publications Ltd,
16 Chalk Hill, Watford, Herts WD19 4BG.